Evening Wind

Evening Wind

Robert Mezey

Wesleyan University Press
Middletown, Connecticut

ABJ -0904

PS
3563
·E98
E8
1987

12/1987
am Le

Some of these poems previously appeared in *Bachy, Backwash, Decal* (Wales), *Gramercy Review, Grove, Iowa Review, Kayak, Marilyn, Missouri Review, New Letters, Poetry Now* (England), *Quarterly West, Spectator, Western Humanities Review,* and *Westigan Review.* "To Be a Giant" and "Of the Power of Thought" originally appeared, in slightly different versions, in *The New Yorker.* The first section of this book, *Small Song,* was originally published in a tiny edition under that title by Humble Hills Press; the third section, *Couplets,* in a somewhat larger edition by Westigan Press.

I wish to thank the John Simon Guggenheim Memorial Foundation and the National Endowment for the Arts for fellowships during which much of this work was done, and the American Academy and Institute of Arts and Letters for an award that gave me additional time and freedom. And I am grateful to Pomona College for many acts of generous support.

LIBRARY OF CONGRESS CATALOGING-IN-PUBLICATION DATA

Mezey, Robert.
    Evening wind.

    (Wesleyan poetry)
    I. Title. II. Series.
PS3563.E98E8   1987   811'.54   86-32462
ISBN 0-8195-2149-3 (alk. paper)
ISBN 0-8195-1150-1 (pbk. : alk. paper)

All inquiries and permissions requests should be addressed to the Publisher, Wesleyan University Press, 110 Mt. Vernon Street, Middletown, Connecticut 06457.

Distributed by Harper & Row Publishers, Keystone Industrial Park, Scranton, Pennsylvania 18512.

Manufactured in the United States of America

FIRST EDITION

WESLEYAN POETRY

for Judah and Naomi
for love is strong as death

Contents

To a Minor Poet of the Anthology

Where now is the memory of the days
that were your days on earth, that spun the thread
of luck and grief and were, for you, the world?

They were swept away in the measurable torrent
of years. You're a word in an index.

To others the gods gave everlasting laurel,
inscriptions on coins and obelisks, avid biographers;
of you, my obscure friend, we know only
that one evening, you heard a nightingale.

Among the asphodel of the shades, your meager shade
will feel that the gods have been ungenerous.

But the days are a tangle of commonplace miseries,
and what better luck than to be the ash
of which oblivion is made?

On other heads the gods have poured
the relentless light of glory,
that peers into the hidden and picks out flaws,
glory, that ends by ruining the rose it adores—
to you, brother, they have shown themselves more merciful.

In the ecstasy of a dusk that will never be night,
you hear the voice of Theocritus' nightingale.

after Borges

Small Song

Let Iddo praise the Lord with the Moth—the writings of man perish as the garment, but the Book of God endureth forever.

The Fields of the Dead

I

Walking all afternoon the fields of the dead
I stopped where the grass flared thick
under an oak, and leaned on a stone
to rest from the high sun.
I sat there cooling in my sweat,
tracing the worn lines, names and years
and little graven images that harvest shadow.
The names near dazed me.
In the still air they seemed to rise
above the stone like heat waves,
and Solomon entered me
still mourning Abigail,
mourning Samuel, Jesse, John,
none of whom lasted a year,
and finally Iris, wife to Solomon, also mourning,
Gone But Not Forgotten.
Not quite yet.
All around, the small slabs sunken in the grass
and a few mansions, grey and innocent.
I felt a road running beneath where I lay.

Time. The buzzing of flies
in the silence.

Clouds piling up, a breeze, sun almost down,
and in its slant of light
I saw the slope
bursting with graves,
graves and evergreens and all the summer's greens,

even cut flowers breathed in a new light.
I rose from my grassy mound and walked a ways
into the freshening garden.

2

It is night.
I am standing outside the low stone wall of the kingdom,
an iron spike under my palm, dust
under my feet. Well, I can't help it,
it *is* dust,
and I can't help pressing my hand against the point.
Looking for miles down the empty road,
arc lamps at intervals throwing brief pools on the darkness,
I can almost see to the end of my life,
almost beyond. . . .

Small Song

Someone lies down alone
In the arms of the new moon,
Someone I think I must know
If I had eyes to see.

What use to pretend we are free
While everything groans not so?
There are these wingless shoulderblades,
These heavy feet on the earth.

Little Poem

Thick spriglets of mistletoe
Asthmatic laughter
Even disease is beautiful
When the eyes are open

On the Burning Coast

to which he comes as often as he can
grandmother sits
waiting for him with thin hands

hands that over eighty years
grasped at everything
slowly opening into a final sculpture

she has forgotten
the sacred embroidery the country dances
even the prayers intended for these moments
her dead husband
everything
all she has is a few dollars
for the fee

evening mingles tenderly with the horizon
putting out all fire

it's like a fairy tale she says
isn't it Alex

and hobbles off across the beach
to join the misty figure
who stands knee deep in the breaking surf

Four-Part Psalm

1

All phantoms of the day
Nothing burns or pierces this dense fog
Ghost of the table
Ghost of the typewriter
Past and future mutilate the appetite

2

I have my name
For the whole shambling charade
Enter and exit
Tentative changeling imperious swineherd morning

3

Nothing expounds
Father and motherandchild
Vestures of empty space swaying here or there
Time sits high
On a throne of calcium

4

Debris of the void
Debut of the blind dancer
We too
Blind dancely hands outstretched
Even as the door opens
A little wind
Even as the oak
All its arms lifting cups of light to the zenith

Twilight under Pine Ridge

Earth between two lights,
one just now draining away
from tiny trees on the western shoulder,
and one to come,
as the stars begin to open in the field of night.
On every slope great trees are flowering
in beautiful relation and yet
all solitary. In the early darkness
clear voices leave off
and fold inward toward sleep.
The grass
parts.
Lord God slides forward on his belly.

Good Fortune by Black Mountain

Late night full moon
black mountain rising pale and massy
the congregation of the trees
share their silver bread

most stars have hidden themselves in moonlight
a few stand shy
like children on some lonely farm

black mountain
one could sleep in its shadow
one could sleep on its full breast
and wake in the milky night
happy

and these rocks
glowing like phosphorus of another planet

they have made you a rich man

To Be a Giant

Hard, hard,
to be a giant,
especially here
where there are few
and one goes crazy.
Should he catch a glimpse
of the little people
running in the fields below,
their hats falling off,
it is all he can do
to keep from crying.
On white hot days
he wanders the hills
of yellow grass,
eating saplings
and stray calves,
ignoring the pains
in his belly. He carries
a small pocket mirror
in which he sometimes
looks at pieces
of his enormous face
and sometimes holds it out,
flashing the commandments of the sun
to the empty hills.

Last Days in Salt Lake City

Dwarfed by a building that would have delighted Mussolini,
A blonde shape hardens in the bright mist.

It's the Angel Moroni, resplendent in gold drag,
Calling the faithful to shop at the Company Store.

Faces heavy as concrete, catatonic faces,
The lost tribe, getting more and more lost.

The radio says make Jesus your business partner
At 10% and the Christ can suck hind titty.

I came here to muse on a bone in the Jewish graveyard,
And the banks locked arms with their cousins the
        mausoleums.

And the last malcontent poet to pass this way
Was detained in front of the wall of a firing squad.

Did you hear that, feet? I won't think less of you
If you leap to a hasty conclusion and split for the coast.

Unsent Letter to Luis Salinas

It's hot in the foothills now even at night
and soon you will be in Texas
sweating the sun and seeking the virgin in Mexican bars.
Obsidian eyes that see the human
and the inhuman with the same anguish,
hands of broken wheat,
bones worn down to frail shadows,
all the weariness of the poor
burns clearly through raw alcohol.
I think of you pushing a heavy brown breast to your mouth
as if you could get away for just one night,
just twenty minutes.
Stay with her, brother, laughing, wakeful,
showing your bad teeth—
while you slept,
they stole your country again
and while they steal,
the bed creaks with the weight of the whole world.
May you have many children,
and the gringos none.

The Silence

How many times God will remember
the silence of the beginning,
that silence which even God himself couldn't endure,
which was finally to blame for our being here now—
he lost his head, and clawing at the earth, picked up some
    mud and made us.

And thus ended the silence,
and then began the howling,
interrupted now and then by a faint chattering
when we make love in our sleep.

One of You

There are some men who have deserted life,
who finally couldn't stand the taste
and spit it out. Something in them is broken
in such a way that only death can heal it,
or worse.
          Sometimes you see one in a Mexican village
walking aimlessly, regarding creation
with a slack stare while all around him sit
the small dark inhabitants of the place,
taut bellies, eaters of suffering. One night
he walks for hours, out past the lighted doorways
and faint snatches of incomprehensible speech
to where the darkness is total and the life
he wanted to remember breathes in the grass
which he can't see. He gets down on his knees
and weeps a little and on his hands
and loses it and finally falls asleep.

In the morning he will order breakfast, hands
curled on the spotless linen, dry face
facing the empty sunlight—but it's the meal
after the last and you will not recognize him.
He is back, and he is one of you again.

Trying to Begin

Here you are once more, sitting at a table,
hands folded and ankles crossed, the most
ordinary of mornings and absolutely nothing to do.
And slowly, neither awake nor asleep,
you start to feel
you must have been lost a long time in the cells of paper,
a faint tinkle of dust
coming back to life in the world of the ear.
The coffee is cold,
yet always the same white ground and the same ghostly
    figures
weaving toward a distant light,
and lines groping for some opening in the crushed wall,
and lines that glisten like the snail's whereabouts
down to this wet sheaf
that might have just arrived, so heavy and fresh,
from the wheat farmers in regions of ice and cloud.
Or maybe just a layer of sodden leaves
left on the doorstep by the nightlong rain.

The Stream Flowing

I remember the creek that ran beside the golf course,
slow and black over rocks; patches of snow;
withies of willow streaming out in the wind,
born to it and, I imagine, bowing and scraping.

I would sometimes sit there shivering and looking out
at the flagless frostbitten greens, the naked trees
that bordered the bleak fairways and a sky
the ashen color of longing and disappointment.

Early winter, it was. And then I remember
the girl I brought there one night—the summer after?
We lay deep on the grassy bank, almost hidden,
and I touched her warm secret hair for the first time.

I can still hear the sound of water pushing by us,
the sound of her breath in my ear as I touched her there,
my stiff boyish hand trembling against her belly.
Her name was June. I could feel a pulse where I touched.

There were little lights in the breathing darkness around us.
Her eyes were closed and I was looking past her
at nameless summer stars and pulsing fireflies
and what must have been houses far off in the night
    somewhere.

Nothing else happened there. We were afraid,
and lay in the matted crush of the maidenhair
and chilly rivergrass. We could smell the night
and see the willow cascading over our heads.

I remember the last time I went there, alone and older,
three or four winters later. The clear water
was still flowing, now between snowcovered banks
and white fields stretched away to the hem of the sky.

One day melts into another and into years,
twenty years that flowed on and lost themselves in the sea.
Where is June, and the boy that she held to her body
on that bank once? Well, useless to think of her now,

and useless to think of the boy, by now a man—
each with a husband or wife, in a house far off
in the midst of another life, where I remember
the fern verging that stream and the stream flowing.

The Celebration

1

What if this man with his rough head
His two hands without jewels
Pretended he was a king
Isn't he a king
Who else would you have beside you

2

I took you in the abandoned church
Sweat pouring down
The guests departed
Ghosts gathered around us
Under the mountain
We celebrated with our new love wine
The lock hanging off the door
The door leaning

3

Without you I might have been
With this woman that
I would have been alone
An effigy
Straining to summon a name
One hand half lifted
To the curve of a lost face

4

You lean back into the night of the almonds
In the seventh year a blossom

An Old Story

1

We met at the edge of the city
Where the road heaps its dust and ends dead
And we kept house.

We kept it in two transparent solitudes,
In two vials of alcohol,
In two lockets—

In one, beheaded geese run to the creamery.
In the other, your farm tilts into the sea
And I cannot find you.

I find you where I found you before,
On the hill of the dead,
Under the shadows of the oak

Whose leaves were sacred once.

2

Once we were horses standing in cold grass
Side by side, head to tail,
Barely touching . . .

You know how horses do.
Now we're just people, wondering
Where it went.

Walking in graveyards,
Two or three graves apart,
Or on the bottom of the sea.

3

Let me begin again.

Under mulberries, in late summer,
The three of us sat to look at the full moon
And mountains steeped in moonlight.

Looking, I thought I should live forever
And love you at least that long.
I was wrong.

He, the third person, was our friend
The moon. Light faded on his mouth,
His eyes refilled with darkness.

He's shining again. And we're still here,
Straining against the ropes
As the whiteness spreads in our hair. . . .

Mercy

for Olivia, for Peter

In an orgy of silence the moon rose
And we sat looking up. Then the wind
Swaying the flowers with a gentle force
Broke open its sweetness on our foreheads.

She said a word long since forgotten,
And you listened to the beating of your heart,
And just over the mountain one white cloud
Came lordly in the radiance of the night.

Something always escapes us, but then the air
Was a drug that we three blindly inhaled,
Till we were lost to hunger and suffering
And could not but behold and be beholden.

Mercy, she said. Now I remember.
And we sat quiet, under a listening sky.
For a moment it seemed we held it all in our hands,
Then let it go, and that was the best of all.

A Way of Saying Goodbye

At last the theatre darkens. Nobody's here.
The old whore begins to look young and sexy again,
and the lies that were told, the lies and the sighs lean
out of the balconies, out of the memory of the air.

Wanting to put your finger on the truth,
you lay down beside her awhile, not sure who
but hopeful that in that dark there were two of you,
that you might touch the body and feel its breath—

or else you thought you did, which is not the same thing.
A mist hangs in what little light remains alive,
like the fumes of a drug, the burning up of a leaf,
the inaudible music that accompanies a dead song.

Ill Lit Blues

The lights come on so early on these winter afternoons;
The darkness creeps up early, winter afternoons,
And somewhere a piano is picking out a musty tune.

With less than an explanation you have taken your liberty
And arranged without thinking that nobody else but me
Will be sitting here in the dark like a granite effigy.

Well, no use complaining, there are a million people like me,
And everything as usual is exactly what it must be:
Character is fate, they say—I'm sure that you agree.

And they say love is easy as the turning of a page—
Haven't you heard that, honey?—like the turning of a page?
But they mumble something different in the back rooms of
    old age.

I'm not a first-time loser, I've been down this road before,
And once again I find myself standing outside a door;
But even as I spell it out, I still don't know the score.

Yet the truth is plain as day, love, all you need do is look;
I can see it clear as daylight, saw it in your parting look—
Love is a sudden emptiness like the closing of a book.

Words

We thought a day and a night of steady rain
Was plenty, but it's falling again, downright tireless.
I like it well enough, the mild crackle
In the alleyway, lulling or minatory, either way
Full of the freshness of life. Much like words.
But words don't fall exactly; they hang there
In the heaven of language, immune to gravity
If not to time, entering your mind
From no direction, travelling no distance at all,
And with rainy persistence tease from the spread earth
So many wonderful scents. And they recur,
Delicious to nose and throat. The word cunt
Often recurs, the word more than the thing,
Perhaps because I came to it so late.
Ocean recurs, perhaps for the same reason, and egg,
Horseman and horse manure, bridal, sap,
And lap with its childish and charming delight in rhyme,
And denial describes its orbit, and blight, and transfigure.
And though I'd argue that those smells of earth
Under the rain's long kneading hands
Are sweeter and more ambiguous than any words,
Darkness, one word that does seem to fall,
Falls, and we're back where we started from.

Of the Power of Thought

The rain falls like an army, clattering
on the thin plastic tied to four trees
for a flimsy roof, though not to be despised.
We watch the drenched pines through a veil of water
and wait, feeling left out, as it gets dark.
It rains hard all evening, we can hear it
even over the hiss and crash of the river.
Curled like a toad in my clammy bag I wish
I was home, at my desk,
dry clothes, pen, paper,
old typewriter under the warm lamplight—
and here I am.

Prose and Cons

Oh shit.

Now Proudflesh was the mumbler one mount of that knack of the woods and as such had some streamly impotent duties, among which were life, levity, and the hirsute hole of happiness. So it come as no supplies that he was trod and found giddy of embracing Nurse Tundra around the waste until she is dead. Witch is why we are spectacle in such matters and hesitate to make a funnel incision.

Wants a pond a thyme, a wight rabid set out to sikh for wisdom. Sot high and low, yeast and vest, Donne & Bradstreet, but all he found was an alarmist incidence of boordom that threatened to break out into an academic. Licked into every cran and nooky but all he founded was a spool of thought that streamed to him the very hide of stupidity. Poured over thousands of ledges and testicles, knocked over banks, sang his muzzle into any crevice no matter how juvenile, and emptied at last into the Specific, to lead a rife old age of supreme contempt for the State.

The old man's mouth wattles at the thought of buttery raga-muffins, sunbaked urchins. If only he could land his choppers in the firm white sighs of a young girl, perhaps he would not have to die. Such an old man is called King Leer. When he opens his mouth to receive the Host, hole continence are orphaned.

The Marines have landed on the Island of Langerhans. There was no resistance. Their instructions are to kill everything that movies. They lye in the sand, trying not to movie.

There wince were three brothers, Carbine, Turbine, and Woodbine. Carbine woke in the Disturbed War, doubly clutching his thundermug; throwing his voice under the duress of a passing nursling, he shot weekly and sank into a comma. Turbine, blessed by nun of his brother's talons, lay in weight by the side of the robe, grinding his molecules. Woodbine was listed as missing in axioms. In a distant city, their mother wept. The Lord smiled at his Croatians. (They also Serb who lonely stand in white.)

There is the Cheap Executive and his staph, whose job is to execute. There is the Supreme Cart, dressed in black roads, whose job is to see the executions are perfectly lethal. There is Congress, mostly with secretaries. For the wrest, thugs, thieves, rubber barrens. They dream of going down on the anals of history.

The Cheap Executive comes on television, so to speak. His brows are knitted into a poison rug of ingratiating hatred. His hams clasp each udder as if frozen in strangle. A voice issues from the tomb of the thorax, full of reinsurance. No knead for panic. Not dead in vein. Business as usury. Public orifice. Offal sacrifice. Whirled leadershit.

The dark aegis and the sitting star of vampire. Old mind fields, raffles stacked in the reign, aircraft carrion, a beached wail. Does he still play the mandarin? He contemplates the ultimate pair o' ducks and mutters, Laquer my rare one.

Agassed at his whorible preposition, she waggled out of her skirt with a miniful look and a curt jester. He advanced his tremulous prototype. She inverted her goblet. He swam the straits and narrows, she lewdly winnowed, he knocked at the door drooped in seaweed, she bore wetness to the billowing dunderhead. He owled, she swallowed, they dissipated into thin heir. Absolute, my Absolute! she cried. At this instance he achieved enlightenment, emotionless on his grassy throne, the loins lying at his feat, the lamps gambling in the meadow.

He love her so he give her a domineering. Ho, ho, she cuckled.

There were Patriark and Matriark and Baby Ark. Baby Ark was called Herman Aphrodite. He/she cried him/herself to sleep, crying, Salmon's been leaping in *my* bed. He/she recede gargled messages. Something about a bottle of the sixes. Something about a menstrual show. Something about poker or poke her or polka, accordion to faminist teary. Men sauna in corporal guano.

Our farther, whose art is heavy, hollow bead I name. Die kingpin come, die wheel be dumb, inert as it is uneven. Gibbous this day airedaley bread, and fork over our test-passes as we fuck over them that test-pass against us. For dyin' is the gingham and the flower and the gory, for rubber and rubber. Aye, men.

One light in the black, one young version, snowy, under things, made her bad now lie in it. But who that blackface in the widowpain, who that burnt car kiss—O Black Panzer man, out of site like a black star, and purr maid soddenly real-eyes: she de spoils, she de little pink booty—at the wonder now, the conk and the conqueror root. And he brake and anther, and he tariff her negligence, and he sock the nibbles with his furry tong and he dig his fungos in the squishy grass and he trickle her vassal and bobble her lobotomies till she summer salt and one swallow make him spring, and at lass she throned up bleached and gasping on his sable promontory. For all her nightmare come true and yet she love him yes she do, who plough deep in the agony and teeth shine in the nape and all that blood all over the Lord's white tidbit.

I plunge my legions to the frog, the anointed snakes of Numerica, and slithery public, the bitchy stands, one nation under guard, invisible, with levity and justice for oil.

For years the Centaur had dreamed of election to the Cent. Now umpires of numbers tumble from his west pocket, a fifth a day, twists his skeleton key in the closets of Georgetown. Quick deals in cloaca-rooms, buttonhole, cornhole, secret saddest, best man at marriage of Lana the Free and Homo the Brave, never consomméd. Sum day a lad with bulging precepts and rackety legs will hand him a shoobox, saying, This is for you, Pa Drone. A waxy statute lies in the Rotunda, and the stern feces of the Four Fathers rankle in the gloom.

The Centaur's untensions were strychnine honorable, though she hoist her pedicles and bit him struck her fur thing, things rearly seen now a daisy. He only oysters on the bolster, subdude, lump, drooling Thigh Kingdom Come. With sudden ignition she screams Majority Whip!—he shivs with pleasure. Free Enter Prize!—he fills his pants. You know this Centaur. He like to incinerate that you are his twin brothel.

In the beginning was the beguine, which was gaud. Thus came Jesus Crassus who foundered Chi Chi Chi and rose on the Thursday. Thus came Macher Roger the beer typhoon, staggering on the beck of Dollar Bill, king of demons and ace of space, who in turns bestrides an enormous turdle of whom you may have hurdle. Thus came Funny Money and Falsie Love and their only blubbered son, His In-a-sense. The Angle of Death plays the Angle of Mercy, no contessa. God stands on their wings, trying to dismember his lines. This is the muddle. There is no and.

Couplets

For plucking the feathers from archangels of the heights,
the delicate snowfall with its slender teeth
is sentenced to the weeping of the fountains
and the desolation of the running springs.

For intermingling its spirit with the metals,
for giving away to iron its sunrises,
powerful blacksmiths drag the fire off
to face the consequences on the ruthless anvils.

Towards the cruel attentions of the thorn
as towards the fatal weakness of the rose,
towards the corrosive action of death itself

I see myself hurled headlong, and all this ruin
is not for any crime, or anything
but loving you, only for loving you.

After Hernández

The fruit is gorged with sweetness past all reason
And the flies come in their hundreds.

Doors opening and closing all night long
But never the right one.

And I used to envy Solomon all those women—
If he was wise, he left them to their own devices.

Nectar rises to the nostril frothy and tingling
And thus the bee is trapped.

I know her better than she knows herself—
Love has conferred on me this trivial privilege.

All night I have lain awake pleading with my heart please
Don't do this to me again.

You never stopped to think why it smelled so good
And you never will.

The eyes close gratefully as the moment ripens,
The tongue searches out its desire in the darkness.

And the arms reach to embrace their own rib cage
And a red absence flashes on the walls of the heart.

You've read a thousand books and what do you know?
Was there some membrane between your eye and the page?

You rummage through the alphabet and the blood
For one word through which the world can be seen.

The odor of women, eyelashes, breasts
Drift now in the starry smoke of memory.

Your eyes were open, but then, so are a blind man's.
So are a dead man's.

Mother is almost gone, father, the children hurry off,
Leaves fly, dust, the season changes.

On the path to the village thousands of wildflowers;
In the sunlight, a young girl drawing water from a well.

Why do we never tire of this story
As if we were hearing it again for the first time?

Mouths searching each other for minutes, years,
Warmer and warmer, looking for the hidden word.

Arms and legs intertwined, skin sliding on skin,
The blood rushing joyously into its channels.

The breasts open their eyes in the darkness of palms,
The eyes widen at every little touch.

The fingers brush against the mouth of the womb
In the conversation of the deaf and blind.

Yoked by flesh, shaking, hollering praises,
They rise as one body to the opening.

The shining phallus erupts in a spray of stars
Flying into her night at tremendous speed.

If their eyes became the darkness, they would see,
Flaming in the darkness, their blowtorch auras.

Sperm on her lips, her hair, her eyes closed,
His whole body bathed in the odor of the garden,

Wet, motionless, barely breathing,
They fill slowly with the surrounding darkness.

The memory of joy is emptier than these empty bottles,
The hope of it just as vain.

The fragrance of her cunt is the fragrance of eternal love
That doesn't last a second.

These splendors of eye and tongue are what wine means,
And fire, and the journey home.

Yet the coolness of her smile is a hierarchy of locked doors
Behind which women disport themselves.

A lightburst of bubbles from dark tons of water . . .
A dress waving in wind . . .

After the snow melts, the snow man stands a long time,
Then the snow man melts.

And they that have power to hurt do it.
They do not do the thing they most do show.

You have a fancy name for your state of mind—
It's just a kettle banging in the wind.

The heart wants instruction in the realities
And pain is expert.

If you're lost in the woods, you move in circles.
If you're done with the fire you started, put it out.

The poet sits praising himself over and over,
As if it mattered, as if it could be proved.

The lover regards his pleasures as his by right;
He seizes on them, he thinks *they* were what he was after.

If you really have it, you don't have to think about it,
You're not always looking to make it something special.

Otherwise, the bud blackens, the petals fray into themselves.
You do not go into the feast until you know this.

To conjure what is not there and not see what is
Was only one of your stupendous gifts.

And to vie with another—as if victory
Shone more brightly than our shameless failures.

As everyone says, you're very intelligent.
There must be something wrong with your eyes.

An infant screams in the darkness of the crib;
A man might as well step off the edge of the precipice.

If I were you, as I am in more ways than one,
I'd look into my heart, and keep looking.

Tu Fu says a poet's ideas should be simple and noble.
Better yet if the poet is simple and noble.

She thinks if she puts out, her sainthood will be recognized.
He figures his wit and pathos entitle him to love.

She laughs and cries, showing her small teeth;
He lifts her dress and buries his face in her bush.

She loves somebody else, who doesn't give a shit.
He does too, but that's different.

It was all good clean fun that had no future
And now it doesn't even have a past.

Neither of them is even alive at this point—
There's just me, and you, I suppose, wherever you are.

What a mess, the meat burnt, the sink overflowing,
The kid won't stop crying, he wants his milk.

The bee's so bloated with nectar he can't fly,
Buzzing on his back at the flower's foot.

So many fresh blooms! Summer will never end,
The fucking idiot dances in his euphoria.

The first faint brown nibbles at the edge of a leaf—
Even the city cousin notices such things.

Down an aisle of leafy shade and leafy sunlight,
Growing smaller and smaller, she disappears.

The watcher, shivering, cannot believe his eyes
That this body too should be taken away from him.

The dry husk of a stonefly clinging to a rock
Came apart in my fingers, the wind lifted it away.

Ojos que no ven, corazon que no siente—
The little peasant whispers it over and over.

From a thousand Chinese dinners, one cookie:
Good fortune in love, also a better position.

So much for both. Too many humorless people
Who can't believe that God could have made the cunt.

Maybe he didn't make it. Maybe hydrogen
Made nitrogen and one thing led to another.

Some hold that early man stumbled upon it
While dreaming of the perfect end to a long day's hunt.

But I say only Italians, with their flair for drama,
Could have invented this fragrant envelope.

Let's drink to the Italians, especially Catullus,
Who knew it was no joke but couldn't help laughing.

A tear falls wordlessly into darkness.
Slivers of gold light faint on the threads of her bodice.

And terrible longings that can't name themselves
Burrow down through the soul and end up digging into wood.

Seven numbers want to be sucked off,
A guy named Susan is dying alone in her bed.

And look, foam is drying into webs in the beer glass,
It wants to rejoin the air and be free of all this.

You can't die from it but you wish you could.
And even at this moment, you smell your fingers.

From the bus window, banks of filthy snow,
Vivid winter faces, none of them hers.

There's the one who kisses and the one who offers the
     cheek—
If I'm love's fool, what is she?

Her first resort was to dwell on how young she is—
The younger the more innocent, the bitch.

Why blame her for the glitterings and the scents?
That sensual phosphorescence belongs to no one.

Straining and sweating toward futures that never opened,
You were the favorite slave of your imagination.

Sometimes, in the small hours of the brain,
I feel if I let go of these lines I'd fall to my death.

She's not the only grief, or the heaviest.
I've got ten more right here under my fingernails.

Yet when I turn them over, they're not griefs at all
But far off lights, a town where we might be happy.

We come from the same town. We used to live there
And must have known once what it meant, without asking.

Remember the depths of her eyes and swimming there.
Remember the glistening festivals of her body.

Remember the sudden chestnut mare and the colt
Running out through buckthorn to the high mountain lake

By which we slept. Remember the fullness of the moon
And the mountains drinking in that sea of milk.

Remember the long silences. Remember the flute
Answering to itself high up on the red cliffs.

Remember the rock floored with sun and two immortals
And the white water crashing and frothing in the channel.

And her arms raised to her hair, lifting the small breasts,
The flat belly, legs akimbo, tuft of fur,

The faint shadow of the wings of the dragonfly—
Remember everything. And now forget it.

The hound keeps circling a putrid lump of fur
But after a while, it gets bored and wanders off.

When the flowers are empty, the bee flies straight home
With no more regret than the setting sun.

Stop crying, lover, you were both well served.
When the bill comes in, someone must pay.

A woman gazes after a man, a man after a woman
But their eyes don't meet. They're looking somewhere else.

Stopping on a deserted street, the shock of seeing
Your half-moon face in the black window.

I see the adjective and the noun entwined,
The verb reaching out its hands to them all.

A line of verse advances into whiteness
With long feelers, like a blind man's cane.

It sings about snow, how warm it is in the snow,
But the next line has something entirely different in mind.

It has the man and the woman, or two men,
And it can scarcely bear to say what it sees.

What did you see in those eyes that made you feel shame
And you wouldn't look but turned your face away?

Black branches whipping, rain streaming down the glass,
A lamp burning beside the empty bed.

The sun had almost buried itself in the grass
Before your shadow leapt off into violet space.

And then the earth disappeared, and there was a stain
Blackening and fading in the emptiness.

Millions of stars look down the speechless dark.
Until finally you too lower your eyes.

In the deep street of the dream, I look up,
Trying to make out a woman's face in a black window.

You can't see anything, and all you can hear
Is a black wind going crazy in the branches.

Just wavering points of light in the hills
And off to one side, maybe half a dozen windows.

The face of Jesus, one side of a flowered bedspread,
False teeth drowning in a glass of water.

What would you say, forty or fifty yards?
The wind on my forehead comes from Andromeda.

Another light goes out in the twig-lashed dark;
Not many people sit up all night around here.

She comes slowly out of the bathroom, takes off her robe,
Sits down in front of the mirror, her face crumbles,

Behind her a man about fifty, with dead eyes—

Suddenly I step through the window

Don't be afraid of dying. The glass of water
Is quickly poured into the waiting goblet.

Your face that will be of no further use to mirrors
Grows more and more transparent, nothing is hidden.

It's night in the remotest provinces of the brain,
Seeing falls back into the great sea of light.

How strange to see that glittering green fly
Walk onto the eyeball, rubbing its hands and praying.

Don't be afraid, you're going to where you were
Before birth pushed you into this cold light.

Lie down here, next to Empedocles;
Be joined to the small grains of the brotherhood.

One, that smiles at echoes and knows it is one.
Two, thrilled, terrified, lost in the fog.

The cold sea that stretches between these lovers
Is wider than the gulf between knowing and not knowing.

What's ignorance but another name for time?
"A time when the thought of the eye made me feel cold . . ."

Our foam and frenzy beats its head against the sea wall,
Although, for a moment there, it seemed . . .

It seems it was a drug, or a recollection,
But no images, only an odor, achingly familiar.

The current passing between the tips of the horns
Burns in the pupils, ripples beneath the black hide.

Yet full of bewildered longing we press to the glass
Toward that far off light burning in the middle of nowhere.

As soon as the water strikes the dish,
The bauble falls from our hands.

And the car ploughs the invisible like an arrow,
Rain leaps on the highway in slashed, blinding sheets.

How many times have I driven a thousand miles
Only to find the door locked, the shades drawn.

To be in love—stroking toward the bed of the ocean
Where the deeper you swim, the harder it is to see . . .

The house is a shambles, the eyes a little nauseous,
Yet the sunlight still falls amorously on the rug.

Doing the dishes, I turned into my two hands
And they sang to each other, a little sailor's tune . . .

The needle veers back and forth in the last groove.
The faint sound of that fire consumes the whole night.

Spectral rings on the table, the mother's rings,
Whose young body once flashed in the firelight.

Not a breath stirs the mound of cold ashes
That still feathers the curve of the Beloved's face.

Nothing beholds itself in the gilded mirror,
The silence is imaginary with no one there to hear it.

To be that no one, disappeared forever,
Already dancing in the golden chambers of the hive!

A bud opens in the light of the word *green;*
From thick foliage, the first tentative trills.

The mantis aligns itself with what is before it,
Motionless in the leaf-and-stem meditation.

And what if some poet carved his name in these woods
As in the crumbling stone of a prison cell?

The letters sprout garlands of leaves, crowns of wings,
Overgrowth covers up the last scarred face.

Even that girl we spoke of, in headlong flight
Feels her arms burst into blossom and curl upward.

Even the lips, moving silently . . .

In a field of mustard and grasses, blowing light,
A house, almost beyond the light. Who lives in it?

Mother is resting. On Sunday it is so.
The cat's eyes half close. The mice go by unmolested.

Alighting to sip dew from the cool ruffles
The butterfly bows slightly, folding her wings.

There in a stripe of sunlight yellow as her blood,
Spilled wine, and a thimble lying on its side.

Glimpses given even to those in torment.
Yes. Even in this world.

Evening Wind

Owl

Nightlong waiting and listening, being schooled
To long lying awake without thoughts,
I hear him calling from the other world.
A long silence, and then two flutey notes—
The cry of nobody, but urgent, cool,
Full of foreboding. He's in the cedar tree
Not twenty feet beyond my window sill;
The other world is very far away.
When, towards morning, he ceases, the air seems
More visible, although it's not yet light,
The black sky drained and all our speechless dreams
Fading into thought. Lord of the night,
Thy kingdom in which everything is one,
Come, speak to me, speak to me once again.

Evening Wind

One foot on the floor, one knee in bed,
Bent forward on both hands as if to leap
Into a heaven of silken cloud, or keep
An old appointment—tryst, one almost said—
Some promise, some entanglement that led
In broad daylight to privacy and sleep,
To dreams of love, the rapture of the deep,
Oh, everything, that must be left unsaid—

Why then does she suddenly look aside
At a white window full of empty space
And curtains swaying inward? Does she sense
In darkening air the vast indifference
That enters in and will not be denied,
To breathe unseen upon her nakedness?

Hardy

Thrown away at birth, he was recovered,
Plucked from the swaddling-shroud, and chafed and
    slapped,
The crone implacable. At last he shivered,
Drew the first breath, and howled, and lay there, trapped
In a world from which there is but one escape
And that forestalled now almost ninety years.
In such a scene as he himself might shape,
The maker of a thousand songs appears.

From this it follows, all the ironies
Life plays on one whose fate it is to follow
The way of things, the suffering one sees,
The many cups of bitterness he must swallow
Before he is permitted to be gone
Where he was headed in that early dawn.

Spring Evening, by Walnut Creek

Hey you frogs! You know
A poet name of Bashô?
No? Well, he knows you.

A Serious Note

Staying up late last night,
I opened the screen door
And stepped outside the light
To look for a star or two.
But stars were few to find,
Those I was looking for,
With eyes a little blind
In the too luminous blue
And soft suburban glow;
And the moon's expressionless O
I used to think expressed
Bewilderment and woe
Was merely drifting through
A drifting wrack of cloud
Directly overhead.
An egg in a flimsy nest?
Or a half-covered breast
In its rumpled habitat?
I almost spoke aloud,
Say what you mean tonight,
But light was all it said—
What can I say but light
And reflected light at that?
Let that be my failing.
So, with a sigh, I bent
To earth and undergrowth
Where I stood, inhaling
The breath of leaf and flower
Spread unseen at my feet,
An overpowering scent
That seemed to me, in truth,

My own sweet life in bloom—
As if one could be both,
Sweetness, and all that it meant
To say that it was sweet—
And under the rich perfume
Was something rank and sour.
No, none of this was mine;
There were the shapes of trees,
Cypress and cedar and pine
Motionless in the breeze,
Green to the black power
Against the pale night sky;
And there, as well, was I.
Who heard, I thought, a thrush
Whistling its artless song
In the oleander bush
Or in the cedar tree,
Brilliant, fluent and free
With never a note wrong.
It was a bewitching air.
But thrushes are pretty rare
In this neck of the woods
And most of our neighborhoods—
It must be some other bird.
And suddenly I knew,
Even before it flew,
Just who it was I heard—
Whoever she wanted to call,
Clearly it wasn't me,
For even as she ascended,
The little mockingbird,

On some invisible mission,
One would have had to be blind
Not to see that derision
Was the last thing she had in mind.
In all innocence,
That was how it ended.
And the best joke of all,
A joke at my own expense,
Was to end on a serious note,
One not intended to be
Misunderstood by me,
Out of a mockingbird's throat.

*

In "The bee's so bloated," the Spanish adage means literally, "Eyes that don't see, heart that doesn't feel," and is equivalent to our saying, "What you don't know won't hurt you."

*

The penultimate line of "Remember the depths of her eyes" consists of the second and third lines of a haiku by Karô.

*

I suppose that almost any of the ancients might have served for the last couplet of "Don't be afraid of dying," but Empedocles seemed especially apt because of his images of the continuous dispersal and mingling of all elements, and a strain of physical disgust that one finds in his writings. (The word "brotherhood" was, I decided, the only word that would do; it is not meant to exclude sisterhood.)

*

"One, that smiles at echoes" refers to a Hindu creation story in which the Godhead amuses itself by dividing and getting lost in matter. The sixth line comes from Charles Darwin's notebooks, I have forgotten exactly where.

*

"Evening Wind" is a somewhat fanciful description of Edward Hopper's 1921 etching of the same title.

*

The story synopsized in the first four lines of "Hardy" is generally accepted by the biographers. Thank God for mindful and resolute midwives. Early dawn is a slight exaggeration—it was 8:00 A.M. of a June morning. The subject of the poem, and perhaps the attack to some extent, was suggested by Donald Justice's sonnet about Henry James.

*

"A Serious Note" alludes to and parodies a number of poems by Frost, Keats, Whitman, and other High Romantics.

79

About the Author

Robert Mezey received his B.A. from the University of Iowa in 1959; he also studied at Kenyon College and Stanford University. Before teaching, he held a variety of jobs, from probation officer to advertising copywriter; he is now professor of English and poet-in-residence at Pomona College. He is the author of eight other books of poetry and of several works of translation. He has received the Robert Frost Poetry Prize, a Guggenheim fellowship, NEA and Ingram Merrill fellowships, awards from the American Academy and Institute of Arts and Letters, and a Lamont poetry award. He lives in Claremont, California.

About the Book

Evening Wind was composed in Sabon by G&S Typesetters of Austin, Texas. It was printed on 60-pound Miami Book by Arcata Graphics/Kingsport of Kingsport, Tennessee. Design and production were done by Joyce Kachergis Book Design and Production of Bynum, North Carolina.

WESLEYAN UNIVERSITY PRESS, 1987